## Learning to Read, Step by Step!

**Ready to Read** Preschool–Kindergarten
• big type and easy words • rhyme and rhythm • picture clues
For children who know the alphabet and are eager to begin reading.

**Reading with Help** Preschool–Grade 1
• basic vocabulary • short sentences • simple stories
For children who recognize familiar words and sound out new words with help.

**Reading on Your Own** Grades 1–3
• engaging characters • easy-to-follow plots • popular topics
For children who are ready to read on their own.

**Reading Paragraphs** Grades 2–3
• challenging vocabulary • short paragraphs • exciting stories
For newly independent readers who read simple sentences with confidence.

**Ready for Chapters** Grades 2–4
• chapters • longer paragraphs • full-color art
For children who want to take the plunge into chapter books but still like colorful pictures.

**STEP INTO READING**® is designed to give every child a successful reading experience. The grade levels are only guides; children will progress through the steps at their own speed, developing confidence in their reading. The F&P Text Level on the back cover serves as another tool to help you choose the right book for your child.

Remember, a lifetime love of reading starts with a single step!

*To Violet, may you always dare to dream big,*
*be bold, and shine bright*
*—L. T.P.*

Random House Books for Young Readers
An imprint of Random House Children's Books
A division of Penguin Random House LLC
1745 Broadway, New York, NY 10019
penguinrandomhouse.com
StepIntoReading.com
rhcbooks.com

Library of Congress Cataloging-in-Publication Data is available upon request.
ISBN 978-0-593-81514-4 (trade) — ISBN 978-0-593-81515-1 (lib. bdg.) —
ISBN 978-0-593-81516-8 (ebook)

Manufactured in the United States of America
10 9 8 7 6 5 4 3 2 1

This book has been officially leveled by using the F&P Text Level Gradient™ Leveling System.

The authorized representative in the EU for product safety and compliance is Penguin Random House Ireland, Morrison Chambers, 32 Nassau Street, Dublin D02 YH68, Ireland, https://eu-contact.penguin.ie.

STEP INTO READING®

A BIOGRAPHY READER

# AMANDA GORMAN
## POET and ACTIVIST

by L'Oreal Thompson Payton
illustrated by Laura Freeman

Random House 🏠 New York

Amanda Gorman is
a famous poet
and an activist.
She once read
one of her poems
to millions of people!

Amanda was born
on March 7, 1998.
She grew up
in Los Angeles
with her family.
As a young girl,
Amanda liked to play
and imagine.

Amanda was raised
by her mom, Joan.
Joan was
an English teacher.

Amanda always loved
to read and write.
She started writing
at five years old!

She would sometimes
paint her poetry, too.
It helped Amanda
to express herself.

But not everything
was easy for Amanda.
She often had trouble
saying certain words.

Poetry helped her
to improve her speech.
She never gave up
on her dreams.

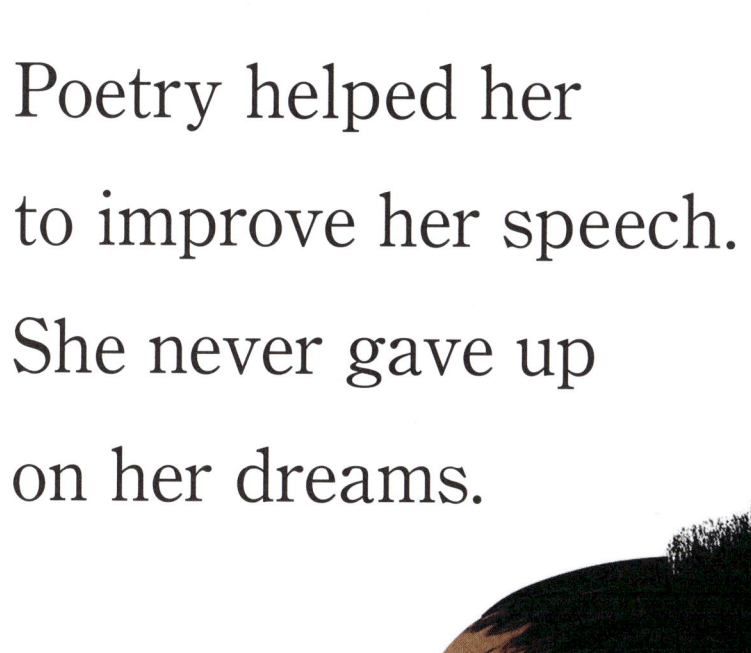

Amanda was chosen
for a special award
as a teen.
She also wrote
her first book
of poetry.

Amanda wanted
to help others.
She started a program
for young people.
Amanda helped them
learn to write.
She believed everyone
could make a
difference!

Amanda received
another award.
It was for poets
who spoke up
for others.
Amanda was
the first person
to ever win this award!

Amanda went
to Harvard University.
She studied society
and culture.

She continued
to write poetry.
Amanda won
many awards
and honors.

Former First Lady

Dr. Jill Biden

was inspired by Amanda.

She chose Amanda
to read a poem
at President Biden's
inauguration.

Amanda was excited.
She wrote and revised
her poem.

She named her poem
"The Hill We Climb."

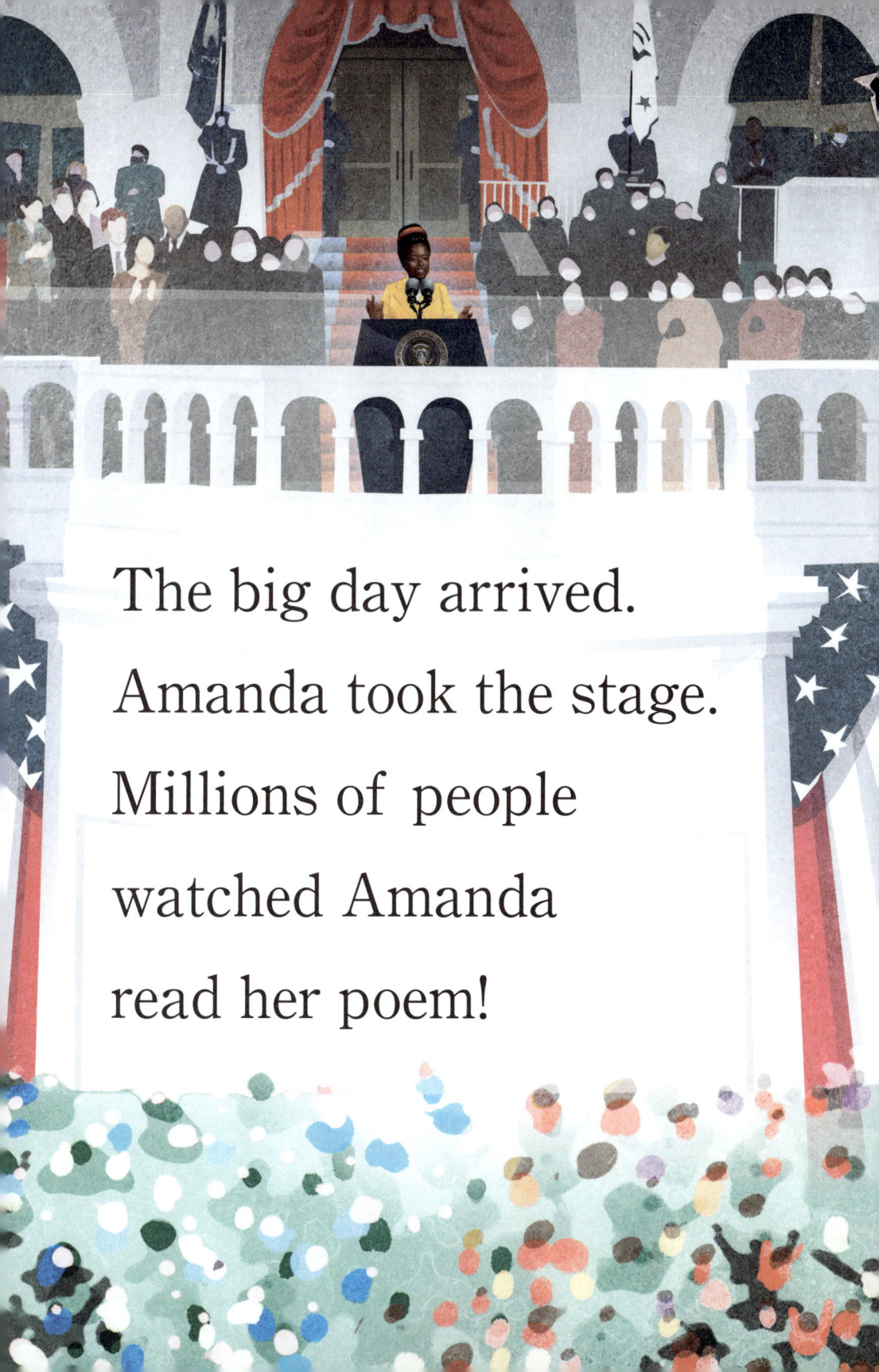

The big day arrived.
Amanda took the stage.
Millions of people
watched Amanda
read her poem!

Amanda spoke about
truth and faith.
She spoke about
history and hope.
She called for unity
and justice
across the country.

Amanda was
on the news
and in magazines
all around the world!

GORMAN SHINES!

VOGUE

VARIETY

AMANDA GORMAN LIVE

YOUNG POET ON HER SHOWSTOPPING
INAUGURAL PERFORMANCE

Now she even writes
children's books!
She also speaks up
about education.

Amanda plans to run
for public office someday.
She will keep working
to change the world.
She wants to inspire others,
especially Black girls,
to lift their voices
and use their gifts.

# How will YOU

# shine your light?